by Iain Gray

79 Main Street, Newtongrange,
Midlothian EH22 4NA
Tel: 0131 344 0414 Fax: 0845 075 6085
E-mail: info@lang-syne.co.uk
www.langsyneshop.co.uk

Design by Dorothy Meikle
Printed by Printwell Ltd

ISBN 978-1-85217-257-2

Gallagher

MOTTO:
Fidelity is my glory.

CREST:
A serpent.

NAME variations include:
Ó Gallchobhair *(Gaelic)*
O'Gallagher
Gallacher
Gallaher
Gallaugher
Goliger

Chapter one:
Origins of Irish surnames

According to an old saying, there are two types of Irish – those who actually are Irish and those who wish they were.

This sentiment is only one example of the allure that the high romance and drama of the proud nation's history holds for thousands of people scattered across the world today.

It's a sad fact, however, that the vast majority of Irish surnames are found far beyond Irish shores, rather than on the Emerald Isle itself.

The population stood at around eight million souls in 1841, but today it stands at fewer than six million.

This is mainly a tragic consequence of the potato famine, also known as the Great Hunger, which devastated Ireland between 1845 and 1849.

The Irish peasantry had become almost wholly reliant for basic sustenance on the potato, first introduced from the Americas in the seventeenth century.

When the crop was hit by a blight, at least 800,000 people starved to death while an estimated two million others were forced to seek a new life far from their native shores – particularly in America, Canada, and Australia.

The effects of the potato blight continued until about 1851, by which time a firm pattern of emigration had become established.

Ireland's loss, however, was to the gain of the countries in which the immigrants settled, contributing enormously, as their descendants do today, to the well being of the nations in which their forefathers settled.

But those who were forced through dire circumstance to establish a new life in foreign parts never forgot their roots, or the proud heritage and traditions of the land that gave them birth.

Nor do their descendants.

It is a heritage that is inextricably bound up in the colourful variety of Irish names themselves – and the origin and history of these names forms an integral part of the vibrant drama that is the nation's history, one of both glorious fortune and tragic misfortune.

This history is well documented, and one of the most important and fascinating of the earliest sources are *The Annals of the Four Masters*, compiled between 1632 and 1636 by four friars at the Franciscan Monastery in County Donegal.

Compiled from earlier sources, and purporting to go back to the Biblical Deluge, much of the material takes in the mythological origins and history of Ireland and the Irish.

This includes tales of successive waves of invaders and settlers such as the Fomorians, the Partholonians, the Nemedians, the Fir Bolgs, the Tuatha De Danann, and the Laigain.

Of particular interest are the *Milesian Genealogies*,

because the majority of Irish clans today claim a descent from either Heremon, Ir, or Heber – three of the sons of Milesius, a king of what is now modern day Spain.

These sons invaded Ireland in the second millennium B.C, apparently in fulfilment of a mysterious prophecy received by their father.

This Milesian lineage is said to have ruled Ireland for nearly 3,000 years, until the island came under the sway of England's King Henry II in 1171 following what is known as the Cambro-Norman invasion.

This is an important date not only in Irish history in general, but for the effect the invasion subsequently had for Irish surnames.

'Cambro' comes from the Welsh, and 'Cambro-Norman' describes those Welsh knights of Norman origin who invaded Ireland.

But they were invaders who stayed, inter-marrying with the native Irish population and founding their own proud dynasties that bore Cambro-Norman names such as Archer, Barbour, Brannagh, Fitzgerald, Fitzgibbon, Fleming, Joyce, Plunkett, and Walsh – to name only a few.

These 'Cambro-Norman' surnames that still flourish throughout the world today form one of the three main categories in which Irish names can be placed – those of Gaelic-Irish, Cambro-Norman, and Anglo-Irish.

Previous to the Cambro-Norman invasion of the twelfth century, and throughout the earlier invasions and settlement of those wild bands of sea rovers known as the Vikings in the eighth and ninth centuries, the population of the island was relatively small, and it was normal for a person to be identified through the use of only a forename.

But as population gradually increased and there were many more people with the same forename, surnames were adopted to distinguish one person, or one community, from another.

Individuals identified themselves with their own particular tribe, or 'tuath', and this tribe – that also became known as a clann, or clan – took its name from some distinguished ancestor who had founded the clan.

The Gaelic-Irish form of the name Kelly, for example, is Ó Ceallaigh, or O'Kelly, indicating descent from an original 'Ceallaigh', with the 'O' denoting 'grandson of.' The name was later anglicised to Kelly.

The prefix 'Mac' or 'Mc', meanwhile, as with the clans of the Scottish Highlands, denotes 'son of.'

Although the Irish clans had much in common with their Scottish counterparts, one important difference lies in what are known as 'septs', or branches, of the clan.

Septs of Scottish clans were groups who often bore an entirely different name from the clan name but were under the clan's protection.

In Ireland, septs were groups that shared the same name and who could be found scattered throughout the four provinces of Ulster, Leinster, Munster, and Connacht.

The 'golden age' of the Gaelic-Irish clans, infused as their veins were with the blood of Celts, pre-dates the Viking invasions of the eighth and ninth centuries and the Norman invasion of the twelfth century, and the sacred heart of the country was the Hill of Tara, near the River Boyne, in County Meath.

Known in Gaelic as 'Teamhar na Rí', or Hill of Kings, it was the royal seat of the 'Ard Rí Éireann', or High King of Ireland, to whom the petty kings, or chieftains, from the island's provinces were ultimately subordinate.

It was on the Hill of Tara, beside a stone pillar known as the Irish 'Lia Fáil', or Stone of Destiny, that the High Kings were inaugurated and, according to legend, this stone would emit a piercing screech that could be heard all over Ireland when touched by the hand of the rightful king.

The Hill of Tara is today one of the island's main tourist attractions.

Opposition to English rule over Ireland, established in the wake of the Cambro-Norman invasion, broke out frequently and the harsh solution adopted by the powerful forces of the Crown was to forcibly evict the native Irish from their lands.

These lands were then granted to Protestant colonists, or 'planters', from Britain.

Many of these colonists, ironically, came from Scotland and were the descendants of the original 'Scotti', or 'Scots', who gave their name to Scotland after migrating there in the fifth century A.D., from the north of Ireland.

Colonisation entailed harsh penal laws being imposed on the majority of the native Irish population, stripping them practically of all of their rights.

The Crown's main bastion in Ireland was Dublin and its environs, known as the Pale, and it was the dispossessed peasantry who lived outside this Pale, desperately striving to eke out a meagre living.

It was this that gave rise to the modern-day expression of someone or something being 'beyond the pale'.

Attempts were made to stamp out all aspects of the ancient Gaelic-Irish culture, to the extent that even to bear a Gaelic-Irish name was to invite discrimination.

This is why many Gaelic-Irish names were anglicised with, for example, and noted above, Ó Ceallaigh, or O'Kelly, being anglicised to Kelly.

Succeeding centuries have seen strong revivals of Gaelic-Irish consciousness, however, and this has led to many families reverting back to the original form of their name, while the language itself is frequently found on the fluent tongues of an estimated 90,000 to 145,000 of the island's population.

Ireland's turbulent history of religious and political strife is one that lasted well into the twentieth century, a landmark century that saw the partition of the island into the twenty-six counties of the independent Republic of

Ireland, or Eire, and the six counties of Northern Ireland, or Ulster.

Dublin, originally founded by Vikings, is now a vibrant and truly cosmopolitan city while the proud city of Belfast is one of the jewels in the crown of Ulster.

It was Saint Patrick who first brought the light of Christianity to Ireland in the fifth century A.D.

Interpretations of this Christian message have varied over the centuries, often leading to bitter sectarian conflict – but the many intricately sculpted Celtic Crosses found all over the island are symbolic of a unity that crosses the sectarian divide.

It is an image that fuses the 'old gods' of the Celts with Christianity.

All the signs from the early years of this new millennium indicate that sectarian strife may soon become a thing of the past – with the Irish and their many kinsfolk across the world, be they Protestant or Catholic, finding common purpose in the rich tapestry of their shared heritage.

Chapter two:
The warrior king

County Donegal, in the northwest of the Emerald Isle, is where the ancient roots of the Gallaghers of today can be found.

A clan with an illustrious royal pedigree, the name stems from Gallchobhair, who is thought to have lived in about the middle of the tenth century.

The name is thought to mean 'foreign helper', or 'helper of the foreigner', derived as it is from 'gall', meaning stranger, and 'chobhair' meaning to aid, or assist.

Gallchobhair was himself a direct descendant of Conall Gulbhan, or Gulban, the fourth son of the celebrated Niall Noíghiallach, better known to posterity as the great warrior king Niall of the Nine Hostages.

The dramatic life and times of this ancestor of the Gallaghers are steeped in stirring Celtic myth and legend.

The youngest son of Eochaidh Mugmedon, king of the province of Connacht, his mother died in childbirth and he was brought up by his evil stepmother Mongfhinn who, for reasons best known to herself, was determined that he should die.

She accordingly abandoned him naked on the Hill of Tara, inauguration site of the Ard Rí, or High Kings, of Ireland, but he was found by a wandering bard who took him back to his father.

One legend is that Mongfhinn sent Niall and his four brothers – Brian, Fiachra, Ailill, and Fergus – to a renowned prophet who was also a blacksmith to determine which of them would succeed their father as Ard Rí.

The blacksmith, known as Sitchin, set the lads a task by deliberately setting fire to his forge.

Niall's brothers ran in and came out carrying the spear-heads, fuel, hammers, and barrels of beer that they had rescued, but Niall staggered out clutching the heavy anvil so vital to the blacksmith's trade.

By this deed, Sitchin prophesied that Niall would be the one who would take on the glorious mantle of kingship.

Another prophetic incident occurred one day while Niall and his brothers were engaged in the hunt.

Thirsty from their efforts they encountered an ugly old woman who offered them water – but only in return for a kiss.

Three of the lads, understandably repelled by her green teeth and scaly skin, refused. Fiachra pecked her lightly on the cheek and, by this act, she prophesied that he would one day reign at Tara – but only briefly.

The bold Niall, however, kissed her fully on the lips. The hag then demanded that he should now have full sexual intercourse with her and, undaunted, he did so.

Through this action she was suddenly transformed into a stunningly beautiful young woman known as Flaithius, or Royalty, who predicted that he would become the greatest High King of Ireland.

His stepmother Mongfhinn later tried to poison him, but accidentally took the deadly potion herself and died.

This legend relates to what was known as the Festival of Mongfhinn, or Feis na Samhan (the Feast of Samhain), because it was on the evening of October 31, on Samhain's Eve, that the poisoning incident is said to have taken place.

It was believed for centuries in Ireland that, on Samhain Eve, Mongfhinn's warped and wicked spirit would roam the land in hungry search of children's souls.

The Festival, or Feast, of Samhain, is today better known as Halloween.

Niall became Ard Rí in 379 A.D. and embarked on the series of military campaigns and other daring adventures that would subsequently earn him the title of Niall of the Nine Hostages.

The nine countries and territories into which he raided and took hostages for ransom were the Irish provinces of Munster, Leinster, Connacht, and Ulster, Britain, and the territories of the Saxons, Morini, Picts, and Dalriads.

Niall's most famous hostage was a young lad known as Succat, son of Calpernius, a Romano-Briton who lived in the area of present day Milford Haven, on the Welsh coast.

Later known as Patricius, or Patrick, he became renowned as Ireland's patron saint, St. Patrick, responsible for bringing the light of Christianity to the island in the early years of the fifth century A.D.

Raiding in Gaul, in the area of Boulogne-sur-mer in

present day France, Niall was ambushed and killed by one of his treacherous subjects in 405 A.D.

Through their descent from Niall, the Gallaghers were members of the tribal grouping known as the Ui Neill, while through their descent from his son Conall they were also part, along with the O'Donnells, Dohertys, Boyles, and others, of what was known as the Cenéal Conail – the kindred of Conail, or Conall.

County Donegal was then known as Tir Chonaill, or Tir Conaill, and the Gallaghers flourished in the barony of Tir Hugh, near Ballyshannon, in the south of the present day county, the barony of Raphoe in the east, and the barony of Banagh in the southwest.

But what proved to be the death knell of the ancient way of life of native Irish clans such as the Gallaghers was sounded in the late twelfth century with the Cambro-Norman invasion of the island and subsequent consolidation of power of the English Crown.

Twelfth century Ireland was far from being a unified nation, split up as it was into territories ruled over by squabbling chieftains who ruled as kings in their own right – and this inter-clan rivalry worked to the advantage of the invaders.

In a series of bloody conflicts one chieftain, or king, would occasionally gain the upper hand over his rivals, and by 1156 the most powerful was Muirchertach MacLochlainn, king of the O'Neills.

The influential Rory O'Connor, king of the province of Connacht, opposed him but he increased his power by allying himself with Dermot MacMurrough, king of Leinster.

MacLochlainn and MacMurrough were aware that the main key to the kingdom of Ireland was the thriving trading port of Dublin that had been established by invading Vikings, or Ostmen, in 852 A.D.

Dublin was taken by the combined forces of the Leinster and Connacht kings, but when MacLochlainn died the Dubliners rose up in revolt and overthrew the unpopular MacMurrough.

A triumphant Rory O'Connor entered Dublin and was later inaugurated as Ard Rí, but MacMurrough was not one to humbly accept defeat.

He appealed for help from England's Henry II in unseating O'Connor, an act that was to radically affect the future course of Ireland's fortunes.

The English monarch agreed to help MacMurrough, but distanced himself from direct action by delegating his Norman subjects in Wales with the task.

These ambitious and battle-hardened barons and knights had first settled in Wales following the Norman Conquest of England in 1066 and, with an eye on rich booty, plunder, and lands, were only too eager to obey their sovereign's wishes and furnish MacMurrough with aid.

MacMurrough crossed the Irish Sea to Bristol, where he

rallied powerful barons such as Robert Fitzstephen and Maurice Fitzgerald to his cause, along with Gilbert de Clare, Earl of Pembroke, also known as Strongbow.

The mighty Norman war machine soon moved into action, and so fierce and disciplined was their onslaught on the forces of Rory O'Connor and his allies that by 1171 they had re-captured Dublin, in the name of MacMurrough, and other strategically important territories.

It was now that a nervous Henry II began to take cold feet over the venture, realising that he may have created a rival in the form of a separate Norman kingdom in Ireland.

Accordingly, he landed on the island, near Waterford, at the head of a large army in October of 1171 with the aim of curbing the power of his Cambro-Norman barons.

Protracted war between the king and his barons was averted, however, when the barons submitted to the royal will, promising homage and allegiance in return for holding the territories they had conquered in the king's name.

English dominion over Ireland was ratified through the Treaty of Windsor of 1175, under the terms of which Rory O'Connor, for example, was allowed to rule territory unoccupied by the Normans in the role of a vassal of the king.

But the land was far from unified, blighted as it was with years of warfare and smarting under many grievances.

There were actually three separate Irelands.

These were the territories of the privileged and powerful

Norman barons and their retainers, the Ireland of the disaffected Gaelic-Irish such as the Gallaghers who held lands unoccupied by the Normans, and the Pale – comprised of Dublin itself and a substantial area of its environs ruled over by an English elite.

A simmering cauldron of discontent and resentment had been created – one that would boil over periodically in subsequent centuries with particularly dire consequences for the Gallaghers and other native Irish clans.

Chapter three:

Riders on the storm

The O'Donnells through time became the most powerful of the tribal groupings of the Cenéal Conail to which the Gallaghers belonged, and both the glorious fortunes and the equally tragic misfortunes of both clans became inextricably linked.

The Gallaghers performed no small role within the ancient Kindred of Conail, granted the rare privilege of attending the sacred inauguration ceremonies of the O'Donnell chieftains and providing the main force of the feared O'Donnell cavalry.

Action for the Gallagher cavalry was certainly not lacking in the aftermath of the consolidation of power over the island by the English Crown.

One indication of the many grievances under which native Irish clans such as the Gallaghers suffered can be found in a desperate plea sent to Pope John XII by Roderick O'Carroll of Ely, Donald O'Neil of Ulster, and a number of other Irish chieftains in 1318.

They stated: 'As it very constantly happens, whenever an Englishman, by perfidy or craft, kills an Irishman, however noble, or however innocent, be he clergy or layman, there is no penalty or correction enforced against the person who may be guilty of such wicked murder.

'But rather the more eminent the person killed and the higher rank which he holds among his own people, so much more is the murderer honoured and rewarded by the English, and not merely by the people at large, but also by the religious and bishops of the English race.'

This appeal to the Pope had little effect on what became the increasingly harsh policy of the occupying English Crown against the native Irish such as the Gallaghers.

But resistance did not only take the form of written appeals.

In 1494, for example, William O'Gallagher was killed during the O'Donnell siege of the Anglo-Norman stronghold of Sligo Castle.

Discontent had grown over the policy known as 'plantation', or settlement of loyal Protestants on lands previously held by the native Irish. This policy had started during the reign from 1491 to 1547 of Henry VIII, whose Reformation effectively outlawed the established Roman Catholic faith throughout his dominions.

This plantation continued throughout the subsequent reigns of Elizabeth I, James I (James VI of Scotland), Charles I, and in the aftermath of the Cromwellian invasion of the island in 1649.

Rebellion erupted in 1594 against the increasingly harsh treatment of the native Irish and its forefront was the O'Donnell chieftain Aodh Rua ÓDomhmaill, better known to posterity as Red Hugh O'Donnell.

In what became known as the Cogadh na Naoi mBliama, or the Nine Years War, Red Hugh and his skilled Gallagher cavalry literally set the island ablaze in a vicious campaign of guerrilla warfare.

The Gallaghers were truly 'riders on the storm' as, under the inspired leadership of Red Hugh, they wreaked a whirlwind of devastation on English settlements and garrisons in a daring series of lightning raids.

In 1596, allied with the forces of Hugh O'Neill, Earl of Tyrone, Red Hugh and his Gallagher cavalry inflicted a defeat on an English army at the battle of Clontibert, while in August of 1598 another significant defeat was inflicted at the battle of Yellow Ford.

As English control over Ireland teetered on the brink of collapse, thousands of more troops, including mercenaries, were hastily despatched to the island and, in the face of the overwhelming odds against them, Red Hugh and the Earl of Tyrone sought help from England's enemy, Spain.

A well-equipped Spanish army under General del Aquila landed at Kinsale in December of 1601, but was forced into surrender only a few weeks later, in January of 1602.

Resistance continued until 1603, but proved abortive.

As the Gallaghers sought refuge where they could, their cavalry dispersed, Red Hugh O'Donnell had already been forced to flee to Spain, where he died in 1602 – at the hands, according to some sources, of an English-hired assassin.

It was not only on the battlefield that the Gallaghers gained a reputation that has ensured them a place in Irish history.

Seven bearers of the surname have been bishops in the barony of Raphoe, in the Gallagher homeland of Co. Donegal.

One of them was Seamus Ó Gallchobhair, born in 1681, and who in later life was also bishop of Kildare. He incurred the wrath of the authorities by insisting on preaching to his flock in the Irish tongue, and his sermons were later collected and published as *Sermons in Irish Gaelic*.

Arguably the most famous Gallagher involved in ecclesiastical affairs, however, was Redmond O'Gallagher, the bishop of Derry who was born in 1521 and who became a martyr through his selfless involvement in the rescue of shipwrecked survivors of the Spanish Armada in September of 1588.

The 130-strong Spanish fleet, intent on the invasion of England, was scattered in heavy storms after its defeat at the battle of Gravelines, and many vessels were driven towards the west coast of Ireland.

This caused alarm on the part of the English authorities on the island, who feared, not without justification, that the disaffected native Irish would rally to their rescue.

William Fitzwilliam, Lord Deputy of Ireland, even sanctioned the use of torture against survivors, while also ordering that anyone who came to their aid would be declared traitors.

At least 24 Spanish vessels are believed to have been

wrecked on the Irish coastline – from Co. Antrim in the north of the island to Co. Kerry in the south.

One of the ships was *La Trinidad Valencera*, which had already taken on survivors of the shipwrecked *Barca de Amburgo*.

Grossly overladen and listing in heavy seas, the order was given to abandon ship as she lay in Glenagivney Bay, in Co. Donegal.

Up to 560 soaked and exhausted survivors managed to make their way ashore, but were intercepted by a heavily armed body of troops.

Trusting to the mercy of the authorities, they had no sooner surrendered their arms when the officers and noblemen were separated from the group and 300 of the ordinary seamen massacred on the spot.

About 150 survivors managed to flee the scene of carnage and, intercepted by sympathetic native Irish, were passed along to Redmond O'Gallagher and Sorley Boy MacDonnell, who hid them for a time before arranging their successful escape to Scotland.

Redmond O'Gallagher paid dearly for his act of mercy – later hunted down and killed as a 'traitor' by English soldiers at Killea, in Co. Londonderry.

Meanwhile, is it only mere coincidence that his proud name, as noted earlier in this brief historical narrative of the Gallaghers, stems from 'helper of the foreigner'?

Chapter four:

On the world stage

Bearers of the name of Gallagher, in all the varieties of spelling of the name, have thrived and continue to thrive in a wide range of pursuits.

Foremost among the Gallaghers of contemporary times who have achieved success in the music field are the brothers **Noel** and **Liam Gallagher** of the British rock band Oasis.

Born in Manchester, the brothers' parents were originally from County Mayo, in Ireland; Noel, the eldest of the two brothers, was born in 1967, while Liam was born in 1972.

With Noel as a guitarist and the band's main songwriter and Liam as the front man, Oasis were at the forefront in the 1990s of what became known as Britpop.

Their first album, *Definitely Maybe*, released in 1994, holds the record as Britain's fastest selling debut album of all time.

Known as much for their controversial antics and comments off stage as they are for their musical talent, the brothers have frequently been involved in highly public squabbles with one another, not to mention the occasional punch-up!

Born in Ballyshannon, County Donegal, in 1948, and of

a rather more retiring nature than the Gallagher brothers, **Rory Gallagher** was the highly influential blues and rock guitarist who formed the three-piece band Taste in 1966.

Pursuing a solo career in the 1970s that saw the release of albums such as *Blueprint* and *Calling Card*, Gallagher shied from personal publicity and is reputed to have at one time turned down an offer from the Rolling Stones to join them as their guitarist.

An inspiration to many musicians, Rory Gallagher died in 1995.

In the world of acting **Helen Gallagher**, born in 1926 in New York City of an exotic mix of English, Irish, and French descent, is the actress, dancer, singer, and makeup artist best known for her role in the American television soap opera *Ryan's Hope*, that ran from 1975 to 1989.

As an award winning Broadway actress she appeared in shows that included *Make a Wish*, *High Button Shoes*, and *Sweet Charity*, while in 1952 she won a Tony Award for her work in the musical *Pal Joey*.

She was nominated for no less than five Daytime Emmy Awards for her work on *Ryan's Hope*, while in 2003 she received a Daytime Emmy nomination for Outstanding Achievement in Makeup in a Drama Series for her work on *Guiding Light*.

Born in San Francisco in 1873, **Edward Gallagher** was one half of a popular vaudeville act known as Gallagher and Shean.

His wife, Helen, was a former dancer with the Ziegfield Follies and she, along with Jack Solomon were responsible for what has now become the franchise known as **Gallagher's Steak House**.

The first restaurant opened next door to New York's Alvin Theatre, on Broadway, in 1933 and it was here that the famed 'New York Strip' steak was first served.

Born in 1985 in Queens, New York, to an Irish-American father and a Cuban-American mother, **David Gallagher** is the actor best known for his role in the American television series *7th Heaven*, while **Jonathan Gallagher Jr.** born in Wilmington, Delaware, in 1984 is the musical theatre actor who is also a recipient of a prestigious Tony Award.

An actress whose television credits include *L.A. Law*, *E.R.* and *Millennium*, **Megan Gallagher** was born in 1960 in Reading, Pennsylvania, while **Peter Gallagher**, born in 1955 in New York City, first achieved acclaim for his role on Broadway in 1989 in Steven Soderbergh's *sex, lies, and videotape*.

In addition to a role in the television series *The O.C.* he has also appeared in a number of films, including *While You Were Sleeping* and *American Beauty*.

In the world of comedy **Leo Gallagher**, born in 1947 in Fort Bragg, North Carolina, is the American comedian who is rather bizarrely best known for smashing watermelons as part of his act.

In the world of broadcasting **Dan Gallagher**, born in 1957 and who died in 2001, was not only a popular presenter of television music shows but also a stadium host of Toronto Argonaut games at the celebrated SkyDome.

In the world of sport **Bernard Gallacher**, born in 1949 in Bathgate, Scotland, is the golfer who has played in the Ryder Cup eight times and was the non-playing captain of the European team in 1991, 1993, and 1995.

Taking up the sport at the tender age of eleven, he won the Scottish Amateur Open Stroke Play Championship in 1967, the same year that he embarked on his highly successful professional career.

Winner of the Scottish Professional Championship on three occasions, Gallacher is now a player on the European Seniors Tour; his first senior win was in 2002 when he took the Mobile Cup.

His daughter, **Kirsty Gallacher**, born in Edinburgh in 1976, has also pursued a career in sport as a successful television sports and radio presenter, while she also frequently gains the accolade of being voted one of the 'sexiest women' in an annual poll for a British men's magazine.

Back on the golf course **Jim Gallagher**, born in 1961 in Johnstown, Pennsylvania, is the professional golfer and sports caster who was a member of America's victorious Ryder Cup team in 1993 and the President's Cup team of 1994.

His brother Jeff and sister Jackie are also golf professionals while his wife, **Cissye Gallagher**, is a former tour player.

On the athletics field **Jackie Gallagher**, born in 1967, is the Australian triathlete and long-distance runner who became both the world triathlon champion and the world duathlon champion in 1996 – the first person to win both titles in the same year.

She is married to the Australian Olympic archery champion Simon Fairweather.

Born in 1903 in Bellshill, Lanarkshire, **Hughie Gallacher** was the Scottish football player of the 1920s and 30s who, as a member of the famous 'Wembley Wizards', beat England by five goals to one at Wembley Stadium, London, in 1928.

Capped nineteen times for Scotland, the talented forward scored a total of twenty-two goals for his country.

Gallacher, who played for a number of Scottish and English clubs, committed suicide in 1957.

In the highly cerebral world of chess, **Joseph Gallagher** is the British Chess International Grandmaster and former British champion who was born to Irish parents in 1964.

Winner of the British Chess Championship in 2001, and the Swiss Chess Championship in 2004 and 2005, he is also an author on various aspects of what is known as chess opening theory.

In the world of literature **William Davis Gallagher**, born in 1808 in Philadelphia, was a noted American essayist and poet, while **Stephen Gallagher**, born in 1954 in Salford, Lancashire, is the British writer whose work includes not only novels but scripts for the highly popular *Doctor Who* television series.

Born in 1945 **Catherine Gallagher** is the esteemed literary critic who, at the time of writing, is professor of English at the University of California, in Berkeley, while **Delia Gallagher**, born in San Francisco in 1970, is the journalist and expert on Vatican affairs who, at the time of writing, is a correspondent for CNN.

In the world of politics, **Willie Gallacher**, born in Paisley, Scotland, in 1881 and who died in 1965, was one of the famous 'Red Clydesiders', who campaigned on a socialist agenda for the rights of the ordinary man and woman.

A trades union activist, he was a founder member of the Communist Party of Great Britain and was imprisoned for a time in 1916 because of his vociferous opposition to the First World War.

He entered Parliament in 1935 as the Communist MP for West Fife.

In the world of business **John Gallagher**, born in 1916 in Winnipeg, Manitoba, was the Canadian petroleum geologist and entrepreneur who founded Dome Petroleum in 1950.

The company was later sold to oil giant Amoco, but Gallagher later founded another company, Prime Energy.

A holder of the office of the Order of Canada and a member of the Canadian Petroleum Hall of Fame, he died in 1998.

Known as 'the grandfather of the disability movement', one particularly selfless Gallagher was **Hugh Gallagher**, the author and international disability advocate who was born in 1932 in Palo Alto, California, and who died in 2004.

He contracted polio at the age of 19 and later went on to campaign for legislation to aid the disabled, including America's Architectural Barriers Act of 1968, that requires all buildings built with federal funds should be so designed that they are accessible to the disabled.

Key dates in Ireland's history from the first settlers to the formation of the Irish Republic:

circa 7000 B.C.	Arrival and settlement of Stone Age people.
circa 3000 B.C.	Arrival of settlers of New Stone Age period.
circa 600 B.C.	First arrival of the Celts.
200 A.D.	Establishment of Hill of Tara, Co. Meath, as seat of the High Kings.
circa 432 A.D.	Christian mission of St. Patrick.
800-920 A.D.	Invasion and subsequent settlement of Vikings.
1002 A.D.	Brian Boru recognised as High King.
1014	Brian Boru killed at battle of Clontarf.
1169-1170	Cambro-Norman invasion of the island.
1171	Henry II claims Ireland for the English Crown.
1366	Statutes of Kilkenny ban marriage between native Irish and English.
1529-1536	England's Henry VIII embarks on religious Reformation.
1536	Earl of Kildare rebels against the Crown.
1541	Henry VIII declared King of Ireland.
1558	Accession to English throne of Elizabeth I.
1565	Battle of Affane.
1569-1573	First Desmond Rebellion.
1579-1583	Second Desmond Rebellion.
1594-1603	Nine Years War.
1606	Plantation' of Scottish and English settlers.
1607	Flight of the Earls.
1632-1636	Annals of the Four Masters compiled.
1641	Rebellion over policy of plantation and other grievances.
1649	Beginning of Cromwellian conquest.
1688	Flight into exile in France of Catholic Stuart monarch James II as Protestant Prince William of Orange invited to take throne of England along with his wife, Mary.
1689	William and Mary enthroned as joint monarchs; siege of Derry.
1690	Jacobite forces of James defeated by William at battle of the Boyne (July) and Dublin taken.

1691	Athlone taken by William; Jacobite defeats follow at Aughrim, Galway, and Limerick; conflict ends with Treaty of Limerick (October) and Irish officers allowed to leave for France.
1695	Penal laws introduced to restrict rights of Catholics; banishment of Catholic clergy.
1704	Laws introduced constricting rights of Catholics in landholding and public office.
1728	Franchise removed from Catholics.
1791	Foundation of United Irishmen republican movement.
1796	French invasion force lands in Bantry Bay.
1798	Defeat of Rising in Wexford and death of United Irishmen leaders Wolfe Tone and Lord Edward Fitzgerald.
1800	Act of Union between England and Ireland.
1803	Dublin Rising under Robert Emmet.
1829	Catholics allowed to sit in Parliament.
1845-1849	The Great Hunger: thousands starve to death as potato crop fails and thousands more emigrate.
1856	Phoenix Society founded.
1858	Irish Republican Brotherhood established.
1873	Foundation of Home Rule League.
1893	Foundation of Gaelic League.
1904	Foundation of Irish Reform Association.
1913	Dublin strikes and lockout.
1916	Easter Rising in Dublin and proclamation of an Irish Republic.
1917	Irish Parliament formed after Sinn Fein election victory.
1919-1921	War between Irish Republican Army and British Army.
1922	Irish Free State founded, while six northern counties remain part of United Kingdom as Northern Ireland, or Ulster; civil war up until 1923 between rival republican groups.
1949	Foundation of Irish Republic after all remaining constitutional links with Britain are severed.